Contents

Part One: Getting to Know You

Activities to break the ice or warm the relationship with your employees

The BIG Book of
LEADERSHIP
GAMES

Quick, Fun Activities to
Improve Communication, Increase Productivity, and
Bring Out the Best in Your Employees

Vasudha K. Deming

McGraw·Hill

*New York   Chicago   San Francisco   Lisbon   London   Madrid   Mexico City
Milan   New Delhi   San Juan   Seoul   Singapore   Sydney   Toronto*

9 0   DOC/DOC   0 9

ISBN 0-07-143525-5

Illustrations copyright © Vasudha K. Deming and licensors.

McGraw-Hill books are available at special quantity discounts to use as premiums and sales promotions, or for use in corporate training programs. For more information, please write to the Director of Special Sales, Professional Publishing, McGraw-Hill, Two Penn Plaza, New York, NY 10121-2298. Or contact your local bookstore.

This book is printed on acid-free paper.

Part Four: Productivity Boosters
Activities to encourage higher productivity

Part Five: Help Them Help You

Activities to help you delegate responsibilities and empower employees

Part Six: Out of the Clear Blue Sky

Activities to tap your employees' creativity and innovation

Part Seven: Knowing When to Follow
Activities to gain insights on leadership from your employees

Part Eight: What You Say and What You Don't

Activities to improve your team's verbal and nonverbal communication

Part Nine: Just for Fun

Activities to alleviate stress and increase fun in the workplace

Part Ten: On Your Own
Solo activities for the leader to do

Introduction

There is nothing quite like the satisfaction that comes from helping other people to learn, to grow, and to perform at their best. And whether you're a manager, supervisor, or trainer, you're continually faced with opportunities to do just that with the employees of your team or organization. My hope is that this book will be of valuable assistance to you in your efforts to be a strong, caring, and effective leader.

People can be motivated to work through the use of any number of incentives: rewards, sanctions, money, fear, competition, and so forth. But a truly healthy and productive workplace puts a different motivator in place: self-actualization (even if that label is not necessarily used). The truth is, people *love* to learn new things, develop their skills, and transcend their previous achievements. It's an intrinsically rewarding human experience. Additionally, the enthusiasm that comes through discovery and development doesn't end in childhood. Adult learners like to "play" as much as children do; they just need a different type of game.

There are any number of ways you can use these games: as stand-alone training activities, as warm-ups to a more intensive training session, or in combination with one another to constitute a comprehensive training event. Alternatively, you can use these games at staff meetings, Friday-afternoon discussion groups, brown-bag lunches, and anywhere else you see fit. (You don't even have to tell employees it's "training"!) Some of the games are designed to take place during business-as-usual; there's no need to find the time and place to facilitate them.

The Big Book of Leadership Games aims to help you do the following:

- Introduce an element of fun into the workplace while still achieving meaningful learning or development objectives.

- Inspire and guide your employees to do their best work.

- Bring out—or optimize—your employees' creativity, innovation, and joy of discovery.

- Create a positive, unified, and upbeat work climate.

- Gain valuable insights into the character, values, motivations, and hidden talents of your employees.

- Develop your own skills and leadership style.

Of course, one book of 50 games is not the only thing you'll need in order to achieve these aims. But it's a place to start— or a place to continue. So, good luck and have fun!

"A good leader is perfect
Only if he is ready to follow
When necessity demands."

—*Sri Chinmoy*

How to Use This Book

This book contains 50 games—long and short, simple and complex—that address 10 key aspects of leadership. Each game is straightforward and easy to deliver. Following is my advice to you for getting the most out of this book and for getting the best out of your employees.

Tips for Success

- Take the time to thoroughly review each game before facilitating it. The better you understand the objective, flow, and tone of each game, the more successful it will be for your group.

- Keep in mind that these are *games*. If you maintain a playful, enthusiastic approach, you'll find that the participants will feel comfortable and motivated to partake.

- Whenever possible, tie the games to real-life examples of situations, trends, and issues at your organization. This will help participants to transfer the learning to their on-the-job environment.

- Play the role of facilitator rather than teacher. The most effective learning comes when you guide the participants in the right direction and then *they* make the discovery for themselves.

- Adapt the games to the climate and culture in which your employees work. If they respond well to small prizes (such as candy or trinkets), then go ahead and use the prizes as rewards at the conclusion of a game. If your employees can be trusted to have fun-spirited competitions (as opposed to heated battles), then turn some of the games into competitions.

- Except for a few props, I've given you everything you need to successfully facilitate the games. Nevertheless, I encourage you to be creative in expanding upon the games in any way that will make them more meaningful and helpful for the participants and for your organization.

- Most of the games easily lend themselves to further discussion and review. Follow up on what participants learned by debriefing after the game, creating changes to the status quo, or establishing a plan for ongoing practice and review.

Part One

GETTING TO KNOW YOU

Activities to break the ice or warm the relationship with your employees

1

A Great Moment

In a Nutshell

Employees describe great moments in their personal or professional lives. This activity serves both to inspire the employees and to give the manager valuable insights into their personalities and values.

Time

About 10–15 minutes (or slightly longer if the group is large). This should be done in a group session.

What You'll Need

A small trophy (usually available in toy stores or party goods stores). Each employee will need a pen and a copy of the handout.

What to Do

Tell employees, "All of us have had great moments in our personal and professional lives, but I'll bet many of us have never heard what great moments have been experienced by the people we work with day in and day out. Now is our opportunity to share those highlights with one another."

Distribute the handouts and give employees about 5 minutes to complete them. Choose someone to start, and hand that person the trophy. Once the first person has finished telling the group about his or her great moments, that employee should pass the trophy to someone else. Continue until everyone has had a turn.

Tip for Success

■ You can start the game by sharing great moments from your own life. Since you are at least one notch above your employees on the professional ladder, be careful to share an experience that comes across as inspiring—rather than arrogant—to them.

A Great Moment

Take a few minutes to reflect on two great moments of your life—
one personal and one professional.

1. Briefly describe your great moments.

    Personal: _____

    _____

    Professional: _____

    _____

2. Name at least three emotions that you felt strongly at each of
    those moments.

    Personal: _____

    _____

    Professional: _____

    _____

3. How did you celebrate or otherwise honor your great moments?

    Personal: _____

    _____

    Professional: _____

    _____

4. How have your great moments changed your direction or your
    perspective?

    Personal: _____

    _____

    Professional: _____

    _____

2

Alphabet Improv

In a Nutshell

In this variation of a popular party game, manager and employee have a spontaneous conversation by beginning each statement with a particular letter of the alphabet. This game is very unpredictable and always fun. It stimulates quick thinking and helps to establish an easy rapport.

Time

5–10 minutes

What You'll Need

Nothing

What to Do

Decide on a suitable scenario. Here are some suggestions:

- You play the role of a customer, and your employee plays the role of an employee who has direct contact with customers.

- The employee plays the role of a manager while you play the role of an employee.

- Both of you play the role of customers who are talking to one another about your company's products or services.

  Alternatively, you can choose to entirely remove the scenario from the workplace environment. Following are a few additional ideas:

- You can be an entertainment journalist interviewing an actor (the employee).

- You can both be historical figures (not necessarily from the same era).

- You can be side-by-side commentators for a sporting event, a dog show, or a live news event.

  Once you've decided on a scenario, decide who goes first and then begin. Encourage the employee to play quickly and spontaneously rather than to think too much about what to say. The same goes for you!

  Here are a couple of examples:

  Salesperson: **A**ll next week, our products will be on sale.
  Customer: **B**et that will be a busy week! . . .

  Manager: **A**ttuning ourselves to the needs of our customers is crucial.
  Employee: **B**ut how exactly do we do that? . . .

Additional Ideas

- Have employees play this game with one another. It works well as an energizer and as a stress reducer.

- Solicit ideas for different scenarios from your employees.

- Use this game whenever you suspect an employee is having difficulty broaching a particular subject with you. It breaks the ice and inevitably serves to "safely" convey some of the employee's feelings about the topic.

3
Emotional Review

In a Nutshell

In this activity, participants use a range of emotions as prompts to share information. It works well as an icebreaker and can be used to introduce the manager to the group or to share information among all participants.

Time

10–20 minutes

What You'll Need

A flip chart and a marker

What to Do

Ask the group to brainstorm several emotions, and write each one on a flip chart. Typical responses are happiness, anger, sadness, fear, and surprise, but the game will be more interesting if you can also get some less generic emotions (exhilaration, confusion, pride, etc.). Be sure to get a mix of positive and negative emotions.

Alternatively, you can choose the emotions and prepare the flip chart ahead of time. You might want to draw a face to accompany each emotion.

Go down the list of emotions and tell participants what specific event has caused you to feel that emotion in the last few weeks or months. If the group is small, have everyone take a turn. If there are more than five employees, however, draw names or ask for volunteers. (After about five rounds, the excitement of the game tends to diminish.)

Tips for Success

- Use this game during new employee orientation.

- Use it when you're new to the group.

- Rather than have everyone go one right after another, spread the "emotional reviews" out over the course of a long meeting or training session. Before and after each break, for example, have someone take a turn.

4

Facts of My Life

In a Nutshell

Employees take turns telling stories about themselves—only parts of which are true. This is a great icebreaker for a group whose members are not very familiar with one another; it also works well as a fun energizer for employees who *do* know each other fairly well.

Time

About 10–20 minutes, depending on the number of employees. This game is designed for a group session.

What You'll Need

Flip-chart paper, markers, masking tape, and one copy of the handout for each participant

What to Do

Give each employee a piece of flip-chart paper, a copy of the handout, a marker, and some tape. Go over the directions with the group:

The aim of this game is for everyone to have some fun telling his or her "story," some of which will be true and some of which will be false! You'll have 5 minutes to write down five to seven interesting facts about your life, but be sure to make at least some of these "facts" false. There's no rule about how many have to be true and how many have to be false—just be sure to put at least one of each in the mix. Write down your interesting "facts" on the flip-chart sheet and post it on the wall. But keep your page covered by taping the bottom to the top until it's your turn to reveal "the facts of your life."

After about 5 minutes, go around the room and have each person share his or her "facts," while others try to guess what's true and what's not. Once everyone has guessed, the person should reveal which ones are the *true* facts.

Tip for Success

■ Create your own "facts of my life" flip chart before the group session and reveal it before asking employees to reveal theirs. Employees will likely have a lot of fun guessing about your life.

Facts of My Life

The aim of this game is for everyone to have some fun telling his or her "story," some of which will be true and some of which will be false! You'll have 5 minutes to write down five to seven interesting facts about your life, but be sure to make at least some of these "facts" false.

There's no rule about how many have to be true and how many have to be false—just be sure to put at least one of each in the mix. Write down your interesting "facts" on the flip-chart sheet and post it on the wall. But keep your page covered by taping the bottom to the top until it's your turn to reveal "the facts of your life."

5
Autodidacts Anonymous

In a Nutshell

Employees share information about what they have taught themselves in the past and what they plan to teach themselves in the future.

Time

Typically, about 10–15 minutes, but possibly longer if the group is large. This is a great activity for a group session, but it can also be done as part of a get-to-know-you-better conversation between manager and employee.

What You'll Need

Nothing

What to Do

Tell employees: "All of us are autodidacts to some extent. Who can tell me what that term means?"

Field answers. The simplest definition is "a self-taught person." Continue by telling employees: "Throughout our lives, we've taught ourselves many things—both consciously and unconsciously. Take a few minutes to reflect on when you've been an autodidact in the past and also what you would like to teach yourself in the future. Then each of you will take a turn sharing with the rest of us."

After about 5 minutes, choose one person to start. He or she should stand up, face the group, and say, "My name is _____ and I'm an autodidact." Then the participant should share his or her autodidact experience from the past and autodidact plans for the future. Continue until everyone has had a turn.

Additional Idea

■ Ask if anyone knows of any famous people who were self-taught.

Part Two
A GREAT PLACE TO WORK

Activities to create a positive work environment

6

Good Enough

In a Nutshell

This is a simple game that illustrates the point that sometimes it's OK to settle for "good enough" rather than to hold out for perfection.

Time

About 15 minutes. This is a group activity.

What You'll Need

A watch with a second hand (or a stopwatch), a flip chart, markers, and tape. Participants will need pen and paper.

What to Do

Note: You can decide whether or not to tell participants to remove their shoes for the first activity. It tends to be a little more effective without shoes because participants can really feel how the muscles in their feet brace against the floor in order to balance. However, be aware that in some groups it may not be appropriate to ask people to remove their shoes.

Ask the group to stand up and face the front of the room. They should keep their legs together, ankles and knees touching one another. Tell them that you're going to time them for one minute as they try to balance perfectly on their two feet and hold absolutely still—they should try not to sway even a millimeter. To help them concentrate, they should remain silent for the minute. Time them for one minute and then briefly discuss the results. No one is able to remain perfectly still for one minute! Nevertheless, if someone had walked by the room and looked in, the viewer would have gotten the impression that—for whatever reason!—the participants were all standing still.

Next, tell participants to take out a piece of paper. They should draw a circle—small or large. Ask them if anyone drew a perfect circle. It's impossible! Yet, if they were to show the drawing to anyone and ask what it is, everyone would say it is a circle.

Tell participants that both of the activities they've just done illustrate the point that sometimes we don't need to be perfect; we only need to be good enough. Divide the participants into small groups and give them 10 minutes to discuss what aspects of work in your department or company have to be only "good enough" rather than perfect.

After 10 minutes, debrief each group as you capture their responses on a flip chart.

Additional Ideas

- Expand the small-group discussion (and the debrief session) to determine when they should not settle for "good enough." What things in the department/organization need to be excellent (or perfect)?

- Briefly discuss with the group the probable results of doing work that's "good enough" but not perfect (when it's appropriate to do so). Typical responses include less stress, higher productivity, better time management, and the like.

7

Made to Order

In a Nutshell

This is a fun, creative activity in which employees write their job descriptions in the style of a retail catalog. The activity helps employees to focus on the positive aspects of their jobs and on the value that they bring to the organization.

Time

15–20 minutes. This can be done either in a group setting or as an individual activity. If employees complete the activity on their own, get everyone together at some point to share the results.

What You'll Need

Several mail-order catalogs. Be sure to get ones that describe the merchandise in detail and that are aimed at a broad consumer base (e.g., a catalog for software will probably be too specialized). Catalogs for clothes, home furnishings, and general gifts tend to work best.

Make photocopies of the handout (one per participant). Participants will need pen and paper.

What to Do

Distribute the catalogs among your employees and tell them to use the product descriptions as a guideline for writing descriptions of their own jobs. Tell them to imagine their jobs as tangible goods—machines or objects—rather than people. They do not have to copy the catalog text; it's just to give them some ideas.

They should write as if they were looking to attract "buyers" to their job. Let them know that, of course, you are *not* looking to replace your employees. This is just a fun game to remind employees of the positive aspects of their jobs and of the value each person brings to the department and the organization. Encourage them not to be modest; they should highlight the key contributions of their jobs.

Distribute the handout with the sample job description to all employees. After about 10 minutes, ask employees to read out their job descriptions, one at a time.

Tip for Success

■ Do this activity yourself—describing your own job—ahead of time and share what you wrote with your employees.

Additional Ideas

■ Allow extra time for employees to draw a picture to accompany the written job description. Have enough colored pens for everyone to share.

■ Collect the job descriptions and bind them together so you'll have a lighthearted catalog of "jobs" in your department. Who knows when this might come in handy?

Made to Order

Sample Job Description

State-of-the-Art Editor: Delight people with the gift of good language. This indispensable gadget allows you to make anyone sound like an intelligent, well-spoken communicator, regardless of his or her true competence. Just drop written text into the "in-box," wait a few minutes, and watch as the Editor magically transforms it into clear, sensible language!

8

Meeting Meddlers

In a Nutshell

Prior to a meeting, the manager secretly gives some participants specific roles to play, all of which can help to make the meeting a more positive experience than it would otherwise be.

Time

This game takes place during an already scheduled meeting. No additional time is required, except for a 2-minute debrief at the end.

What You'll Need

A photocopy of the handout; cut out each of the Meeting Meddler roles.

What to Do

Take a little time to decide which employees would be best suited to play each of the Meeting Meddler roles. Once you've decided, ask each person individually if he or she is willing to play the role. Be sure to tell them that nobody else should know that any meddling is taking place. Make plans to reimburse those meddlers who are bringing something material (treats, flowers, etc.) to the meeting.

During the meeting, give positive reinforcement to the meddlers, as appropriate, but do not let on that there is a conspiracy under way.

At the end of the meeting, ask all participants if they felt that anything seemed different from usual. Solicit answers and then let everyone know that you had previously conspired with a few of the participants to make the meeting more positive and upbeat. Point out that although some of the communication was contrived, this did not make the meeting any less effective or undermine the business purpose of the meeting.

Depending on the general personality of your group, you may or may not want the Meeting Meddlers to identify themselves and tell everyone what role they played during the meeting.

Additional Idea

■ Expand the debrief session to ask participants what else they would like to see happen during a meeting.

Meeting Meddlers

Make a photocopy of this page and cut out the various roles.
Secretly give each role to one of the meeting participants.

Your role during the meeting: At least twice during the meeting, praise someone (for offering an idea, for being well-spoken, etc.)

Your role during the meeting: Use only positive verbs. Avoid such words as *can't* and *won't*. Instead, phrase things positively (*can*, *will*, etc.).

Your role during the meeting: Be an enthusiastic cheerleader. Find opportunities to make emphatic statements such as "We can do that!" or "That would be great!"

Your role during the meeting: Every time someone looks at you, smile.

Your role during the meeting: Bring an unexpected treat—cookies, chocolates, fresh fruit, specialty drinks, or the like.

Your role for the meeting: Before the meeting, without being seen, clean and tidy the room. Put some flowers in a central location in the meeting room.

9

See It and Believe It

In a Nutshell

This activity includes two effective visualization exercises that can be done anytime to encourage employees to maintain a positive self-image and to energetically work toward their goals.

Time

Just a few minutes. This activity should be done first in a group setting, but once employees have learned the techniques, they can do them on their own anytime.

What You'll Need

Photocopies of the handout (one per participant)

What to Do

Tell employees that visualization can be a powerful tool to use in bringing about their success in any endeavor. All good things begin with imagination! Use either or both of the following visualizations as a guide. Speak slowly, calmly, and clearly. Pause at the logical places in order to let people focus on the images. Then let them sit in silence for a minute or longer.

After they've done the visualization, give everyone a copy of the handout so that employees can repeat the visualizations whenever they like.

Visualization 1

Sit up straight and close your eyes. Visualize yourself as a professional who has an important job to perform and who makes a difference in people's lives every day. See yourself walking into the room with confidence and poise. Visualize yourself dressed exactly as you'd like to be seen by others. You're well groomed, smiling, and energized. Imagine yourself interacting positively with your colleagues and enthusiastically approaching your work.

Visualization 2

Close your eyes and call to mind two or three goals that you're working or saving toward. These might be material goals such as a new car or a vacation, or something else such as a promotion or another work-related achievement. See yourself happy and proud—the way you'll feel when these goals have been realized.

Additional Idea

■ Encourage employees to put written or visual reminders (such as pictures) at their workstations to help them keep their goals in mind while they work.

See It and Believe It

Visualization 1

Sit up straight and close your eyes. Visualize yourself as a professional who has an important job to perform and who makes a difference in people's lives every day. See yourself walking into the room with confidence and poise. Visualize yourself dressed exactly as you'd like to be seen by others. You're well groomed, smiling, and energized. Imagine yourself interacting positively with your colleagues and enthusiastically approaching your work.

Visualization 2

Close your eyes and call to mind two or three goals that you're working or saving toward. These might be material goals such as a new car or a vacation, or something else such as a promotion or another work-related achievement. See yourself happy and proud—the way you'll feel when these goals have been realized.

10

Verbology

In a Nutshell

Employees use a list of powerful verbs to stimulate ideas about how their work makes a difference in people's lives. This is a great motivator for employees and helps them to see the value of their hard work.

Time

About 15 minutes in a group session

What You'll Need

A flip chart, a marker, and photocopies of the handout (one per employee). Employees will need pen and paper.

What to Do

Before the session, write the following 10 words on a flip chart:

Elevate

Inspire

Motivate

Impact

Accomplish

Create

Boost

Contribute

Delight

Serve

Tell employees that this list provides 10 of the most powerful and positive verbs in the English language. Because the success of any organization (or team) lies in its ability to achieve these goals—not in what it merely intends to do—the objective of this activity is to identify ways in which your organization succeeds.

Divide employees into small groups and give them 10 minutes to come up with ways in which their work—via the products and services of your organization—achieves these aims for customers, employees, their community, and the world at large.

After 10 minutes, ask each group to report its responses. Distribute the handout to employees and encourage them to focus on accomplishing these actions during the course of their everyday work.

Tip for Success

- If you feel that some other verbs will resonate well with your employees, add them to the list (or substitute them for others).

Verbology

Elevate

Inspire

Motivate

Impact

Accomplish

Create

Boost

Contribute

Delight

Serve

Part Three
ON THE SAME TEAM

Activities to foster collaboration and support

11

Common Values

In a Nutshell

This activity provides a great way for employees to establish some guidelines for a positive and productive work environment, whether that means a brief meeting, a training session, or the everyday work environment. The best part is that since participants come up with the guidelines themselves, they're more apt to follow them than they would be if the guidelines had been imposed on them from management or some other outside entity.

Time

About 10–15 minutes in a group session

What You'll Need

A flip chart and markers for the debrief portion of the activity

What to Do

Try this game first in a meeting or training session (or any group activity that lasts from an hour to a few days). See "Additional Ideas" (on the next page) for other options. Tell employees that the success of any group session depends largely on whether or not the people involved observe the same rules and regulations. Briefly discuss what happens when this does not occur (for example, people become annoyed; the unity of the group diminishes).

The purpose of this game is to come up with some guidelines that reflect common values of the participants. Once the guidelines have been established, all participants will be expected to follow them for the duration of the group session.

Put participants into groups of three or four and tell them that they'll have 5 minutes to discuss some common expectations—things they all agree should be adhered to during the group session. Following are two examples:

- Be on time.

- Participate wholeheartedly.

After 5 minutes, ask each group to announce its results, as you capture the common values on the flip chart. Once something has been suggested by a group, ask one or two people from other groups to say what the benefit or value of that expectation is. For example, if everyone is on time, the class won't be disturbed by latecomers, and nobody will miss any of the presentation/learning. Confirm that everyone in the session agrees that these guidelines should be followed.

Leave the flip chart up for the duration of the session. You might want to take the time during a break to rewrite it neatly and colorfully (or ask an artistic participant to do it).

Additional Ideas

- If you want to expand the activity, you can take time to discuss what will be the results of noncompliance with these common values.

- Try out the same activity, taking a little more time, to create common values for the everyday work environment.

12

Secret Buddies

In a Nutshell

This is an inspiring, simple game in which employees secretly observe one another, focusing on positive, admirable aspects of the character and work of the "secret buddy." The game builds camaraderie and helps team members to see the best aspects of each other.

Time

About 5 minutes for the initial setup. The observation phase of this activity then takes place over the course of one or more days, and the debrief takes about 10 minutes in a group session.

What You'll Need

Index cards (one per participant plus a few extras)

What to Do

Decide ahead of time how long you want participants to observe one another. Typically, the best results come when employees are given a day or two. You should also decide how and when you want to reconvene the participants after the observation period so that they can share the positive things they observed.

Once you're ready to start, pass out the index cards (one per person) and ask everyone to write his or her name at the top of the card. Then collect all the cards and shuffle them. With the names facing down (so that they cannot be seen), spread the cards out in your hand and ask each person to pick one card. Anyone who gets the card with his or her own name on it should put it back and pick again. Otherwise, they should all keep the first card they draw.

Tell the participants not to show anyone their cards and not to tell anyone whose name they have drawn. Explain that their task now is to secretly observe this person and to use the card to write down at least three positive traits about this person's character, work practices, or the like. Tell them how long they will have to make their observations. (The extra index cards are in case anyone wants to start over by writing comments on a new card.)

When it's time to reconvene the group, elect one person to start. That person should stand and face his or her "secret buddy" and tell that person directly what three qualities were observed. The person who just received the feedback goes next, and so on until everyone has had a turn.

Tip for Success

■ In order to teach employees to be comfortable giving and receiving praise, make sure each person addresses the secret buddy as "you," not "he" or "she." And ask each person to say "thank you" after receiving the feedback.

13
Testimonials

In a Nutshell

This is an activity you can do anytime to help capture the positive emotions and strong sense of accomplishment that employees feel after working hard toward a goal.

Time

Approximately 5 minutes for employees to write their testimonials

What You'll Need

Index cards and pens

What to Do

The objective of this activity is to have employees write positive "testimonials" about their experiences during a particular work-related project. At the appropriate time, hand out index cards to employees and ask them to take a few minutes to write about the value of what they've just done. Following are a few questions to get them started:

■ What would you tell others about the experience?

- In what ways have you seen your hard work pay off?

- How has the experience benefited you?

  You can then keep these testimonials on file and use them at appropriate moments in the future. For example, when an employee is feeling frustrated about a project, you might ask the employee to read the testimonial he or she wrote two months earlier after successfully completing a previous project that no doubt had its frustrating moments.

  You can also use the testimonials to inspire employees to try something new. For example, if you've got some good testimonials from employees who previously attended a training session, you can use them to help persuade others to attend the training.

  Following are some times when it's particularly important to capture employees' thoughts and emotions:

- After a successful event (training session, trade show, client meeting, etc.)

- Once a major change has taken effect and the employees have had time to adjust

- After achieving an important goal

- Anytime strong and positive recognition has been received (from upper management, customers, etc.)

Additional Idea

- Collate the testimonials into one document and send it via e-mail to your group of employees (or make a hard copy for them to keep). They'll likely receive further inspiration and insight from reading one another's testimonials.

14
Show and Tell

In a Nutshell

Employees each present a project they're currently working on and describe its value to the team, to the organization, and/or to customers. This game achieves three ends: it keeps your team well informed, it encourages a supportive climate, and it gives employees the valuable experience of presenting in front of a group.

Time

A few minutes per employee

What You'll Need

One copy of the handout for each employee

What to Do

This game requires some planning and preparation on your part. A few days or a week before you want to have the Show and Tell presentation, let employees know when and where you'll hold the group session, and give everyone a copy of the handout. Encourage them to come to you with any questions or concerns when planning their presentations.

If you have several employees working on the same project, either have each of them present one aspect of it or have them show and tell as a group (in which case you may want to give them more time to present).

At the group session, remind employees that *everyone* has done Show and Tell at some point in life—usually in grade school. It was then, and is now, a great way for each person to inform, to inspire, and to learn. Then have each employee show and tell. Following each presentation, ask the group if they have any questions for the presenter.

Tips for Success

■ Be prepared to offer some specific, meaningful praise to each employee after his or her presentation. The praise should be more than a thank-you for the presentation; it should be a testimony—in front of peers—of that employee's value to the team.

■ This is a good opportunity to present your employees with rewards such as an annual bonus or just a thanks-for-all-your-hard-work surprise.

Show and Tell

Plan a brief presentation (3–5 minutes) to "show and tell" a project you're currently working on or have recently completed. In planning your presentation, keep the following in mind:

- Use various media and graphics to make your presentation vivid and interesting.

- Do your best to make it fun, playful, and original.

- Consider using some simple props—a magic wand, a hat, some music.

- Be sure to point out not only *what* you're doing but also *how* that project is making a valuable impact on the team, organization, and/or customers.

- Practice your presentation beforehand so you'll be comfortable with it and so you'll know it's within the appropriate time range.

15

Puzzle Masters

In a Nutshell

Employees work in two groups to complete a puzzle, and each group has to work under different constraints.

Time

15–20 minutes

What You'll Need

Purchase two identical jigsaw puzzles. The puzzle should be of intermediate complexity and have a neutral and inspiring image on it—a nature scene, tropical fish, a cityscape, or the like. You'll also need one copy of the handout, from which you cut the two different sets of instructions, so that each team will have only its instructions.

What to Do

Prior to the Group Session

■ Make sure the session room has two tables large enough for the finished puzzles. It will be best if the tables are round or square (rather than long and rectangular) so that participants can be on all sides of them when completing the puzzles.

Also, the tables should be far enough apart that the two groups can work without being tempted to "spy" on one another through either seeing or hearing.

■ Put the pieces of each puzzle on the tables—one puzzle per table. For now, hide the boxes showing the finished picture.

At the Group Session
■ Divide the group into two teams and give each team its instructions from the handout.

■ Give the puzzle box to Group 1, and ask the members to make sure it cannot be seen by Group 2.

During the session, make sure each group follows the rules. After 10 minutes have elapsed, check to see how much progress each team has made.

Debrief participants following the game by discussing how it felt to (1) attempt to collaborate without communication, and (2) attempt to reach a goal without knowing what that goal is. Discuss any analogies they find between this game and their real-time work environment.

Puzzle Masters

Group 1: Work together to complete the puzzle. Use the picture on the puzzle box as a guide. The people on your team may not speak to one another or write each other notes. Get as much of the puzzle done as you can in 10 minutes. Be careful not to allow the other team to see the picture on the puzzle box.

Group 2: Work together to complete the puzzle. You will not have a picture of the completed puzzle to use as a guide; it's up to you to figure out what it's supposed to be. Collaborate with your teammates as much as possible to make as much progress as you can on the puzzle in 10 minutes. Be careful not to let the other team hear you.

Part Four
PRODUCTIVITY BOOSTERS

Activities to encourage higher productivity

16

The 10-Minute Solution

In a Nutshell

Employees come up with various ways to increase productivity by implementing a daily change.

Time

This can be done in a group setting, in which case 10 minutes is probably sufficient time for participants to come up with their ideas. Results may be better, however, if employees are able to take a day or two to decide individually on what activity they'll do and then report back to the manager.

What You'll Need

Nothing

What to Do

Ask each employee to come up with one action that, if implemented for 10 minutes a day, would have a positive effect on productivity (individual and/or group). It should be something that the employee is willing to commit to doing every day for at least a month. Following are a few ideas:

- Respond to e-mail messages.

- Meditate.

- File paperwork.

- Search for sales leads.

- Do exercises for the eyes, wrists, neck, and back.

- Review reports.

Once they've come up with their ideas, ask them to inform you of what they'll be working on. Then designate a specific time of day for the employees to carry out the actions (or allow them each to choose their own time). Let employees know that they should keep track of their progress and that you'll be convening the group at regular intervals so that they can share results.

For the first day or two, and then again at the beginning of each workweek, remind employees to do their 10-minute activities. (You might want to find a creative way to do this, such as putting up a sign, ringing a bell, or sending an instant message.)

After about two weeks and then again after a month, get the employees together and ask them to report on what they have been doing and how it has helped productivity. You can decide at that point whether they should continue, stop, or change to a new activity.

17

Grid Luck

In a Nutshell

Over the course of a regular day, employees work toward a goal and, once they've reached it, have a chance to try for a prize. To win this game, employees need to have both luck *and* skill.

Time

This game takes place over the course of a regular work shift. The manager does need to do some preparation, however, including buying prizes for the winners. (See What to Do section below.)

What You'll Need

A flip chart or white board, markers, and prizes

What to Do

Prior to a shift, draw a large grid on a white board or flip chart. There should be as many squares as there are employees on your team. If your team is small, allow two squares per employee. Do not assign names to squares—employees will do this themselves during the game. Make an identical but smaller grid on a piece of paper and keep this one to yourself. (See the first sample grid.)

Select a few prizes and write the name of each prize in a separate square on your small grid (but not on the large one). For example, if you have 16 employees (and therefore 16 squares), you might select four prizes and assign them to four random squares.

Designate an individual goal that you're sure everyone will reach at some point during the shift. When an employee reaches the goal, he or she can come up to the large grid and put his or her name in any available square. You should also put the name on your grid. (See the second sample grid.) This continues until all employees have put their names in a square. Toward the end of the shift (or once everyone has met the goal), match the prizes to the employees whose names appear in the corresponding squares and give out the prizes.

Grid Luck

Sample 1

Lottery Ticket			
			Movie Coupons
		Gift Certificate	
			Book

Sample 2

Devon *Lottery Ticket*	Alan	Gia	Luke
Ainsley	Patrick	Paul	Saul *Movie Coupons*
Pierre	Trudy	William *Gift Certificate*	Caroline
Nina	Martha	David	Chanese *Book*

18

Nothing New

In a Nutshell

Employees enjoy a "nothing new" period during which they are able to turn away any new work commitments. This activity can be done on a regular basis to allow employees to catch up on work and to show that you're committed to an equitable workload and pace of productivity.

Time

Time varies. (See What to Do section below.)

What You'll Need

One copy of the handout for each employee

What to Do

Decide ahead of time how long you want the Nothing New phase to last. The feasibility of this activity depends, of course, on the demands of your work environment. Not all work teams can survive a prolonged period of disallowing any new work. Nevertheless, almost everyone can afford to do it for an hour or two, and many work groups can easily accommodate a few days.

This activity conveys a message to your employees that you value their ability to focus on the work they already have without having to deal with a constant influx of new work. It also shows that you want them to experience the feeling of accomplishment that comes with completing tasks.

Inform employees that they're about to enter into a Nothing New phase. Give them each a copy of the handout listing the Rules of the Game.

Let them know both when the period officially starts and when it officially ends. Debrief the activity by asking employees to share stories about what they accomplished and how they felt about being able to say no to new work.

Additional Ideas

- You might want to try an extended but scaled-back phase of Nothing New. For a period of weeks or even months, you can hold off on accepting any new major projects. Once you're caught up, you can again accept new commitments.

- Ask employees to keep track of what they said "no" to during the Nothing New period. Although this might at first seem a little counterintuitive, it actually will help employees to see that they are meeting the objective. Keeping track can be done in the simplest way: just jot a few words onto a notepad each time something new is turned away.

Nothing New

Rules of the Game

During the "Nothing New" phase:

■ You are not allowed to accept new tasks, make new commitments that require your time and energy, or accommodate any requests that were not made prior to the start of the Nothing New period.

■ You should work diligently on commitments that you already have.

■ You can elect not to answer the telephone or respond to e-mail if you're confident that these communications are not related to work you already have.

■ You should politely let people know you're in a "Nothing New" phase if they attempt to give you new work.

19

Tell Me How to Treat You

In a Nutshell

Employees complete a questionnaire that managers can use to gain insights about how to reward employees for their success.

Time

About 10 minutes. This can be done individually or during a group session.

What You'll Need

One photocopy of the handout for each employee

What to Do

Tell participants that they're going to complete a questionnaire. This is their chance to express what types of rewards and recognition are most important and meaningful to them.

Distribute the questionnaires, allow about 10 minutes for employees to complete them, and then collect them. Do not review them as a group.

Review the questionnaires and keep them on file so you can refer to them whenever it's time to reward an employee for a job well done. They'll be delighted to be recognized in a way that is meaningful to them. Take note of each employee's answer to the final question, which asks how they like to be recognized outside of tangible rewards. Put this into practice on a regular basis.

Tips for Success

■ To show that this is more than a fruitless exercise, find opportunities to reward your employees (using their own suggestions) within a few weeks of doing this activity.

■ Because it's likely employees' preferences will change over time, have them complete the questionnaire again in a year or so.

Rewards and Recognition

Name: _____

Date: _____

Following are some questions about what types of rewards and recognition are most meaningful to you. Answer the questions honestly and completely. Nobody but your manager will see your answers.

1. What are some of your favorite hobbies and interests? _____

   _____

2. What are some of your favorite retail stores and online retail sites? _____

   _____

3. What types of rewards are most meaningful to you? _____

   _____

4. What are some "small" rewards that you would be delighted to receive? _____

   _____

5. What are some "large" rewards that you would enjoy? _____

   _____

6. Outside of tangible rewards, how do you like to be recognized for your hard work? _____

   _____

20

Priority Pie

In a Nutshell

Employees take an honest look at how they're spending their time and energy at work, and then have an opportunity to redirect themselves. This activity is a real eye-opener for most people, the end result of which is higher productivity and less employee stress.

Time

About 20–25 minutes (longer if you plan to discuss what steps employees need to take in order to shift their priorities). This activity can be done either in a group setting or as an individual exercise.

What You'll Need

Photocopies of both handouts for each employee

What to Do

Start with a brief discussion about the importance of knowing how much time and energy we're actually putting into the projects we work on. Advantages of this knowledge include the following:

- We can make realistic estimates about how long a project takes from start to completion (and by extension, how much money it costs and how much labor it requires).

- We can avoid the stress and frustration that comes with unrealistic expectations.

- We can learn how to pace ourselves rather than have to frantically work to get something done.

- We can make good on our work commitments to other people.

Tell participants that they're now going to do an activity that will help them to see at a glance where their time goes in a day. First they'll create a pie chart that reflects an actual day, and then they'll create one that reflects how they would *like to be* allocating their time and energy at work.

Distribute copies of the handouts to each employee. Ask them to review the samples and then to complete their own pie charts. In the first one, they should divide the pie to mirror how much time in a typical day they spend on each activity. In the second pie, they should chart how they want to be spending their time and energy at work. (*Note*: Depending on the maturity and character of your group, it may be necessary to point out that, of course, they should *not* fill the second pie with non-work-related activities such as going to the beach or surfing the Internet. This is an opportunity for them to take a serious look at how they can improve productivity and job satisfaction.)

Allow about 15 minutes for employees to complete their charts, and then debrief as you see fit. You may want to review the charts as a group to see where trends or patterns exist.

It helps to follow up this activity by talking with your employees about what steps are necessary to take in order to make their workdays reflect their ideal allocation of priorities.

In a week or two, check with employees to see if they've been able to shift to a more ideal allocation of their time and energy at work.

Additional Ideas

- Rather than do the activity all at once, have employees develop their Priority Pie charts over the course of several days, so that they can give a very accurate, real-time estimate.

- Encourage employees to do this activity for their personal lives as well. They can look at how much time they actually spend (versus what they want to spend) on family activities, spiritual life, hobbies, fitness, recreation, education, and so forth.

- Do this activity yourself, prior to having your employees do it. Consider sharing the results with them. They'll be motivated by your example.

Priority Pies

Sample 1

How You're Really Spending Your Time and Energy:

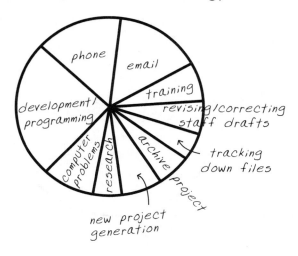

Sample 2

How You Want to Be Spending Your Time and Energy:

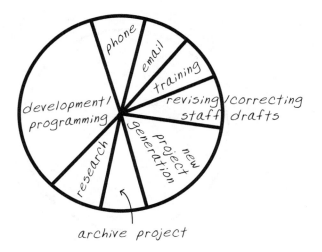

Priority Pies

How You're Really Spending Your Time and Energy:

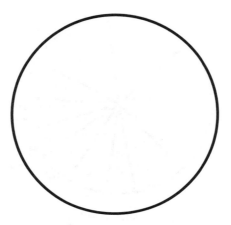

How You Want to Be Spending Your Time and Energy:

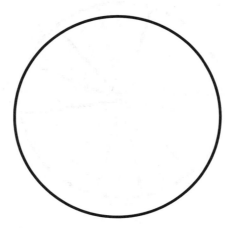

Part Five

HELP THEM HELP YOU

Activities to help you delegate responsibilities and empower employees

21

Problem Solvers

In a Nutshell

This activity helps you to empower employees and transform them from problem reporters into problem solvers. Employees complete a work sheet that helps them to literally be part of the solution.

Time

Time varies. This is an individual activity, but it can be done in a group setting as well.

What You'll Need

Photocopies of the handout. Make several copies to keep on hand so that you'll be ready to give it out whenever an employee comes to you with a problem.

What to Do

You can do this anytime an employee comes to you with a problem. It shouldn't take the place of your actually listening to the employee, but once you've done that, you can follow up by giving the employee a copy of the "Problem Solvers" handout. You can also do this activity in a group session, having employees work alone or in groups to come up with problems and solutions.

Tell the employee who comes to you with a problem to complete the handout and then to give it to you for your review. Once this has been done, give the employee your approval to proceed with solving the problem—or adjust the suggested solution as necessary.

Be sure to tell the employee to follow up with you so that you'll know about the progress/outcome of the issue.

Tips for Success

- Make sure employees describe the problem in objective terms—something stronger and more universal than "I don't like it."

- Remind employees that the simplest solutions are almost always the best. At the very least, they should be applied before more complex solutions are attempted.

Additional Ideas

- Praise employees—in front of their peers—whenever they've successfully set the solution into motion (or solved the problem outright).

- Keep a copy of the completed "Problem Solvers" handouts in employees' files to remind you of their proactivity when it's time for their performance reviews.

- If you want your employees to be less dependent on your assistance, you might want to cover up the last question on the handout before making photocopies.

Problem Solvers

Describe the problem and give some recent, specific examples.

_____

_____

Why is it a problem? In what ways does it detrimentally affect our team, organization, product, or other function? _____

_____

_____

What is the simplest solution you can think of to address this problem? _____

_____

_____

How would that solution take care of the problem? In what ways would it help our team, organization, product, or other function?

_____

_____

What steps are you willing to take to put this solution into motion?

_____

_____

What help, support, or involvement would you like to receive from your manager/supervisor? _____

_____

_____

_____

22

Information Relay

In a Nutshell

In this relay-style activity, each employee has to find a piece of information related to the organization, its customers, or the team itself. At the end of the relay, employees convene to share the information—and to realize that the sum is greater than the parts.

Time

The first leg of this relay is carried out by individuals and can take place over the course of a few days. The subsequent group session takes about 15 minutes.

What You'll Need

Index cards. For the group session, ask each employee to bring a dollar bill (they'll get it back).

What to Do

Part 1—Preparation and Delegation

Inform employees about the activity and make arrangements for the group session, which takes place after everyone has found the information assigned. Prepare questions for the information you want team members to uncover. The questions should meet the following criteria:

1. Finding the information should require employees to do some legwork, but not so much that it distracts them from their other work.

2. The assignments you give to employees should be more than just administrative tasks. The aim of this game is to empower employees and increase their professional knowledge.

3. There should be no trick questions. In other words, make sure the answer does exist and can be found with a reasonable amount of effort.

4. The information to be uncovered and subsequently shared by the employee should be relevant to the job, organization, and/or industry.

   The following are examples, though not necessarily suggestions. You should take the time to come up with useful, empowering questions for *your* employees.

- On average, how many customers does the team serve via phone and e-mail each week?

- How does our organization measure customer satisfaction?

- How many of our direct competitors offer their products internationally?

   Write each of the questions on an index card (one question per card). Hand out one index card to each employee and let employees know that they're expected to investigate the answer, write it on the card, and bring the card to the group session.

Part 2—Group Session

Take out a dollar bill and ask someone to trade it for another dollar bill. Then ask that person to trade with someone else. Continue this several times and then ask the group: "Is anyone richer now that we've exchanged all this money?" Once the employees confirm that no one is richer, point out that if they had exchanged information instead of dollar bills, everyone would be richer for having learned something new. That's what they're going to do now!

Have employees take out their index cards and one by one share the information they found with the rest of the group. Wrap up by pointing out how everyone's individual efforts contributed to the overall enrichment of the team.

23

The Absolutes

In a Nutshell

Employees work together to determine what should and should not be done in the department and/or organization. This activity helps to empower employees and can give the leader valuable insights about what is important to them.

Time

About 15 minutes in a group session

What You'll Need

A flip chart, tape, and markers

What to Do

There are two ways to conduct this activity. You can either have all subgroups focus on the same general topic (e.g., "the Absolutes of this department") or have each subgroup discuss the "Absolutes" for one aspect of the job, team, or organization. For example, you might have one group focus on interpersonal communications, one group focus on customer service, and one group focus on the physical work environment. Decide ahead of time which option you want to do so you'll be prepared to facilitate the activity.

Divide employees into groups of three or four. Give each group two flip-chart pages, some markers, and some tape to post their pages.

Tell employees that their task is to discuss "the Absolutes" and come up with two lists. At the top of the first flip-chart page, they should write "Thou Shalt . . ."; at the top of the second page, they should write "Thou Shalt Not . . . ."

Give groups about 10 minutes to come up with their lists and then ask each group to present them. You might want to have someone type up the lists and circulate copies to all employees.

24

We Hold These Truths

In a Nutshell

Employees follow the lead of the Declaration of Independence by establishing that certain truths are "self-evident." This activity is very empowering and motivating for employees and is perfect to do as a preface to a challenging or lengthy work project.

Time

About 10 minutes. This is a group activity, but it can be altered to be an individual activity if necessary.

What You'll Need

A flip chart and markers

What to Do

Tell participants: "At the very beginning of the Declaration of Independence, Thomas Jefferson wrote, 'We hold these truths to be self-evident' and then listed certain humanistic principles that underlie the establishment of the United States of America. These words, and those that followed, helped to give courage, direction, and confidence to the people who formed the nation.

"Although we may not be establishing a new country, the work we do is important and valuable in its own right. So, in order to help us go forward with our upcoming challenges, we're going to remind ourselves of what we know to be true."

At the top of the flip chart, write: "We hold these truths."

Ask participants to cite important lessons they've learned from their past experiences that can help to motivate them for the future. The things they mention should be positive, empowering, and, of course, true for the whole group. For example, you might lead off by offering one or more of the following "lessons":

- Every tough project *does* eventually reach its completion.

- We constantly grow and learn as we engage in new work.

- The collective knowledge and capacities of our team are enormous.

Note: If you feel that participants might be reluctant to offer individual responses, you might put them in small groups for 5 minutes or so to discuss the "truths" and then ask for a report from each group.

Capture the responses on the flip chart. After the session, ask one of the participants to neatly rewrite the information on the flip chart (or do it yourself). Either keep the flip chart posted in view of employees or give each of them a printed version to keep in their workstations.

Tips for Success

- Purchase a poster-size card-stock "scroll" (available in some office-supply and art stores). At the completion of the activity, transfer the truths from the flip chart to the scroll.

- Rent a Founding-Fathers type of costume to wear when facilitating this activity. At least get the wig!

25

Here's What I Would Do

In a Nutshell

Employees brainstorm creative ideas for serving their internal and external customers.

Time

Approximately 10–15 minutes in a group session

What You'll Need

A flip chart and marker. Employees will need pen and paper.

What to Do

Preface the activity by briefly discussing the concept of internal and external customers. As a group, develop a list of customers—even if they're members of the organization—that are served by this group of employees.

Put participants in groups of three or four. Tell the groups to imagine that they make the rules regarding what could be done for all these customers. Ask them what measures—small or large—they might take to serve their customers better.

Tell participants to be specific and to frame their ideas in a positive way. For example, rather than say, "I wouldn't make them wait on hold so long," they should say, "I would guarantee a hold time of no more than 2 minutes."

Give each group a blank sheet of paper to record their ideas and tell them they'll have only 5 minutes to brainstorm.

After 5 minutes, ask each group to report its results. Capture them on a flip chart. Determine which ideas can be implemented right away and ask participants to put them into practice. For those ideas that require further research and/or approval from senior management, delegate an employee or committee of employees to take the necessary next steps.

Be sure to stay "in the loop" as these changes are researched and implemented, but let your employees take the lead. If some of the changes cannot be implemented, have employees report the reasons to the rest of the group.

26

Brick by Brick

In a Nutshell

Through simulating the completion of some grand-scale projects, employees discover that every project—no matter how large—becomes manageable once it is broken down into smaller tasks.

Time

Approximately 20 minutes in a group session

What You'll Need

A flip chart and markers

What to Do

Ask participants to tell you the biggest task they've ever taken on—at work or outside of it. After hearing from the participants, ask whether they've ever considered what it would be like to have the responsibility for building a skyscraper, planning a city, swimming across the English Channel, composing an opera, or doing something else on an equivalent scale. Tell them that now's their chance to take on that responsibility—but only for a few minutes!

Put participants into pairs or small groups. Assign one of the following tasks to each group and tell employees they'll have 10 minutes to break it down into a manageable step-by-step process. Often this is a multilayered experience: they break down the initial project and then break down those pieces and then break down those pieces, and so on.

Tell participants that they shouldn't worry about not having the industry-specific knowledge required to actually do this task; they should just have some fun and take their best guesses as to what the project entails. Give them one more bit of advice: it's all right if they don't complete the entire breakdown process. They should just make as much progress as they can in 10 minutes.

Tasks

- Build a bridge over a large river.

- Create a set of encyclopedias.

- Organize an expedition to the South Pole.

- Plan a symposium with representatives from 70 countries.

- Run for president of the country.

- Eradicate hunger from the world.

After 10 minutes, debrief participants on the process. (You do not have to hear the details of each group's project.) How did they approach the task? Does it seem manageable now that they see it as simply a series of smaller tasks? Do they or will they apply the "brick-by-brick" process to their own work projects? What happens when they do this (less stress, stronger feeling of accomplishment, increased confidence, etc.)?

Additional Ideas

■ For a variation of this activity, or for a "reminder" round at some later date, have the employees brainstorm several large-scale, seemingly overwhelming projects. Then distribute these, rather than the projects provided in this activity, to the subgroups to break down.

■ Keep the learning from this activity alive by regularly reminding employees to break their work down into manageable tasks—"bricks" or "chunks"—and to focus on just the tasks, not on the overwhelming scale of the entire project.

■ Recognize and reward employees on a "brick-by-brick" basis rather than waiting until the completion of a large-scale project. Of course, you and your team should also celebrate in a big way upon completion of the overall project!

Part Six

OUT OF THE CLEAR BLUE SKY

Activities to tap your employees' creativity and innovation

27

Phictional Philanthropy

In a Nutshell

This is an inspiring, thought-provoking activity in which employees come up with ideas for their own fictional charity or nonprofit organization. The activity gives employees an opportunity to reflect on their values and interests, and it gives managers a unique insight into employees' characters.

Time

If this is done in a group setting, allow 20–30 minutes. If it's done as an individual activity, employees may want a few days to reflect before completing the activity.

What You'll Need

A flip chart, markers, and one photocopy of the handout for each employee. You may also want to gather information on a variety of actual philanthropic and nonprofit organizations to give employees some ideas.

What to Do

Prior to the session, write the following on a flip chart:

Possible causes for your philanthropy:

- *Families, children, or women*
- *Housing*
- *Health care*
- *Education*
- *Peace and justice*
- *Civil rights*
- *Spiritual life*
- *The environment*
- *Financial solvency*

Tell employees that they are going to be given the chance to create a fictional philanthropic organization, the funding for which will come from an anonymous benefactor. Their task is to reflect on the social cause most important to them and to complete the handout.

Encourage employees to be creative and to choose a cause that is close to their hearts. Once employees have finished, ask them all to make a brief oral report to you and the rest of the team.

Additional Ideas

- Ask employees (individually or in small groups) to research some actual charities, foundations, or other nonprofit organizations. Give them copies of the handout and ask them to report back once they've completed the form.

- Have employees work together to come up with a way to put their philanthropy to work within your organization.

Phictional Philanthropy

You have been given the directive to start a foundation, charity, or other nonprofit organization. You have also been given the money necessary to start the organization and to carry out its objectives for one year, assuming that the anonymous benefactor who gave you the money finds your plan worthwhile and reasonable. At the end of one year, your benefactor will decide whether or not to continue funding your organization.

What is the name of your organization? _____

_____

_____

What is its primary aim? _____

_____

_____

What segment of society benefits directly from your organization?

_____

_____

What specific actions does the organization carry out? _____

_____

_____

Who will you choose to sit on your board of directors? _____

_____

_____

28

Job Aid Jamboree

In a Nutshell

Employees work in small groups to come up with job aids that will help the department or organization to work more efficiently.

Time

About 20 minutes

What You'll Need

A flip chart and marker. For the initial setup session, employees will need pen and paper. After that, they will need various materials but will find them on their own (that's part of the game).

What to Do

If you're not doing this as part of an existing group session, convene your employees for about 20 minutes to do the setup for the game.

Discuss the concept of a job aid: It's something that helps people to do what they need to do when they need to do it.

Examples include the instructions and diagrams that appear on the screen of a copy machine and laminated cards showing the shortcuts for various software applications. Job aids come in all shapes, sizes, formats, and materials.

Ask employees to tell you some of the advantages of a job aid. Following are some typical responses. Mention any that aren't cited by the employees.

- They help to increase efficiency.

- They can help reduce errors.

- They teach you something you didn't know.

- They prevent you from having to memorize complex information.

Put employees in small groups and give them 5 minutes to brainstorm a list of other job aids that they have used either at work or outside of it. After 5 minutes, ask each group to present its list.

Tell employees that the next step is to come up with ideas for new job aids that they can create to help everyone in the department (or the organization). Keep employees in their small groups and give them about 10 minutes to brainstorm ideas for new job aids.

After 10 minutes, ask each group for its ideas, and list them on a flip chart. Then, as a group, choose one or two ideas to implement right away. (You can save the other ideas for later.) Come up with an action plan for creating the job aid(s), and put them to use as soon as possible.

Additional Idea

- Hold a contest to see who can come up with the most useful and helpful job aid. Participants should work on their own— not telling anyone what job aid they're developing. Once all the job aids are complete, display them anonymously and allow employees to vote on which are the best ones. After the voting, reveal the name of the winner(s) and give a reward. Most important, make sure that the most useful job aids get produced and distributed to all appropriate employees.

29

Colors for Sale

In a Nutshell

Employees practice their presentation and persuasion skills by competing with one another to win over "buyers." Even if your employees do not formally sell anything, this is a useful activity for helping them to think creatively and to communicate effectively. It is, however, best suited to employees who are adept at making spontaneous presentations and who are comfortable "competing" with others.

Time

Approximately 20 minutes. Time will vary depending on the number of presentations. This is a group activity.

What You'll Need

One photocopy of page 91 cut into strips with one color each. (If you have more than 12 employees in the session, come up with some additional colors. Alternatively, you can select some participants to be a panel of judges.) You'll also need paper, pen, tape, and a clock with a second hand. You might also want to get a couple of prizes for the winner(s).

What to Do

Before employees come into the room, tape one color-strip to the bottom of each person's chair.

Set up the game by telling participants that they'll be competing with one another by making brief presentations. The object is to get the "audience" (the other participants) to select the employee's product over all the others. After all the presentations, the group will vote on who was the most persuasive.

Tell them they'll have 5 minutes to prepare for their presentations and a maximum of 1 minute to present. Finally, let the participants know that they'll each be making a presentation of a color—an intangible product. They can say or do whatever they want to in order to get the audience to choose their color over someone else's. They might start by asking themselves what are the benefits, advantages, and connotations of the color they're representing.

Once they understand what they're supposed to do, tell them to look under their chairs and begin preparing. After 5 minutes, ask someone to make the first 1-minute presentation. Continue until everyone has had a turn, and then hold a vote to determine the winner.

Spend a few minutes debriefing the game by discussing what approaches or techniques were effective in winning over "buyers." How can this be carried over to the real-time work environment?

Colors for Sale

Red

Orange

Yellow

Purple

Green

Brown

Black

Gray

Blue

Tan

White

Pink

30

All the News

In a Nutshell

Employees work together to create a mock-up newspaper that covers various aspects of the organization—and predicts future events. This fun, empowering activity lends itself well to several variations, so it can be done by employees at all levels of the organization.

Time

This tends to be a fairly long activity—typically 45 minutes to an hour. The creativity and collaboration that the activity generates, however, can prove well worth the time invested.

What You'll Need

Photocopies of the instructions in the handout (one for each group of three or four employees). A flip chart and marker, tape, several glue sticks, several pairs of scissors, and about a dozen newspapers (all from different days). You should bring in all the parts of the newspapers, but they don't have to be in order.

What to Do

Prior to the Group Session

There are a number of ways to carry out this activity. If your group is small (fewer than six people), you might want to have everyone work together to create the newspaper. If the group is larger, you can divide participants into two or more groups and have each group create its own newspaper. Alternatively, you can put them in groups of two or three and have each group create just one section of the paper (this considerably decreases the time needed for the activity). Decide ahead of time which option you want to do so that you'll be ready to facilitate the activity.

At the Group Session

Start by asking the group to name the various sections and aspects of a typical newspaper (front-page news, local events, features, sports, obituaries, ads, etc.). Capture the responses on a flip chart as the group calls them out and keep it in view during the activity.

Tell the group that now is their chance to create a newspaper focused on the events of your organization (or department). Not only that, but also they get to do what no newspaper publisher has ever done: create a newspaper of future events. And to make it easy, they have to come up with only headlines rather than full stories.

Distribute the instructions sheet and go over it with the participants to make sure they understand the game. Make the assignments you previously planned, and give each group a flip-chart page, a glue stick, some scissors, and a few newspapers.

Once they've all finished, ask each group to post their newspapers on the wall. Then let everyone walk around and read them.

Additional Ideas

- You might want to debrief participants following the activity by discussing how each group worked together. Did an "editor" emerge? Did they divvy up the work? How did they reach consensus about what to put in their paper? Why did they choose the sections they did, while omitting other sections?

- Have each employee choose *one* headline and write the "full story."

Front Page of the Future

Using a single sheet of flip-chart paper, create a front page that features headlines from the future of your company. Work with your group to carry out the following steps:

- Come up with a name for your newspaper and a date sometime in the future.

- Divide the page into various sections—at least six—and give each section a heading (Sports, Obituaries, News, etc.).

- Discuss with your group what information you would like to put in each section. In other words, what will be going on in our company on the date you have chosen? Have fun, be creative, and think outside the box. For example, an Obituaries section could announce the death of a policy or a problem rather than a person; the Sports section could have headlines that use sports analogies to report on competition with a rival of the company.

- Create only headlines, not full stories.

- Take some time to look through the newspapers and cut out words or phrases you want to use. You are allowed to use only newsprint on your front page; you can't write the headlines by hand. Look for fun, interesting, unusual words and find a way to put them together to convey your meaning.

- Glue the newsprint to your flip-chart page and get ready to announce your news about the future of the organization!

31

Never Been Played Before

In a Nutshell

Using a variety of common game items, employees work in small groups to invent entirely new games for their peers to play. This activity challenges employees to be highly creative, innovative, and quick-thinking. It's best suited to employees who you feel can cheerfully embrace that challenge. Ideally, this activity should be performed by a large group.

Time

Approximately an hour in a group session

What You'll Need

A variety of game items: playing cards, dice, small hourglass timers, gaming chips, play money, tiny plastic or metal figurines, and the like. You should also throw in some common nongaming items such as straws, chopsticks, and balls. You'll need enough for each team to have three types of items, but participants should have plenty of choices, so get more than is strictly necessary. It's also a good idea to bring in some small prizes for everyone—they deserve it after this activity! (Participants will also need pen and paper.)

What to Do

Prior to the session, put the accompanying guidelines on a flip chart or white board, but do not reveal it until the participants know what they'll be doing.

Put all the items on a table in the session room, but don't tell participants what they're for. Divide participants into groups of three or four. Then ask one member of each team to come up to the table and choose three items. (Items such as straws, chopsticks, etc., should be in sets, so that participants will take a set rather than just one item.) Alternatively, you can have each team choose one item at a time, wait for the other teams to go, and then take another item, and so on.

Once each team has *three* items, assign them their tasks. They will have 30 minutes to create a game using all the items they have chosen. Reveal the flip chart and go over the guidelines. You can decide whether you want the games to have some tie-in to work (e.g., players have to answer a work-related question or know certain workplace trivia). If so, let the participants know (and add it to the flip chart).

Encourage the teams to be creative and to have fun, and then give them 30 minutes to invent their games. After 30 minutes, the participants should rotate around the room and play the games. (One person from each team will have to stay behind to administer the game to visiting participants, but team members can rotate this role.)

After everyone has had a chance to play the games, hold an informal vote for the best game. Debrief employees on the activity by having teams discuss how they came up with their ideas, what worked and didn't work, what inspirations came about through working under pressure, and so forth. Tell participants that they *all* deserve a prize and distribute the prizes.

Never Been Played Before

Guidelines for creating your game:

- The game should have a clear, specific objective.

- It should be easy to determine whether a player has won or lost.

- You can choose whether to have your game played by a single player or by multiple players.

- You must use all three of the items you have chosen.

- Your game should involve both skill and luck.

- You must create a set of rules for playing your game.

Part Seven

KNOWING
WHEN TO FOLLOW

Activities to gain insights on leadership from your employees

32

Leadership Haiku

In a Nutshell

Participants come up with haikus to simply and concisely illustrate their perspectives on leadership. This is an intriguing game that yields valuable insights for the manager.

Time

About 10–15 minutes. This is best done in a group session.

What You'll Need

A flip chart and marker and one copy of the handout for each participant. Participants will need pens.

What to Do

Prior to the session, create a flip chart listing the following information:

A poem with three lines
Syllables: five-seven-five
On any topic

Reveal the flip chart and ask the group if anyone can tell you what this is. If nobody knows, explain that this is a haiku describing the art of haiku. A haiku is a traditional form of simple, concise poetry consisting of three lines. The first line has five syllables, the second seven, and the third five. That's what makes a poem a haiku.

Distribute the handouts and ask participants to take a few minutes to come up with haikus of their own on the topic of "leadership." Once they've completed their haikus, ask for volunteers to share theirs. Collect the handouts so you can later review *everyone's* take on the topic of leadership.

Additional Ideas

- Bring in a book of haiku poetry and read a few poems to the group at the beginning of the activity.

- If the group is large, you may want to assign some people to write on alternative—but synonymous—topics such as "management" or "boss."

- Do another round in which employees create a haiku on the subject of "success."

Leadership Haiku

A haiku is a traditional form of simple, concise poetry consisting of three lines. The first line has five syllables, the second seven, and the third five. Take a few moments to reflect, and then write your haiku in the space below.

33

Every Which Way to Lead

In a Nutshell

Employees brainstorm leadership qualities and then reveal which ones are most important to them. This is a great way for managers to get insight into which leadership styles work best with their employees.

Time

About 15 minutes. This is a group activity.

What You'll Need

A flip chart and marker, tape, and stickers. The stickers can be any kind, but it adds an element of fun to the activity if you have a variety of colorful, playful stickers (cartoon characters, flowers, dinosaurs, animals, cars, etc.). You'll need enough stickers for each employee to have two, but purchase more than this so employees can have a choice.

What to Do

Start by having each employee choose two stickers from the supply you brought in. Then divide the employees into groups of three or four and ask each group to brainstorm "the qualities of a leader." Tell them to think of a variety of leaders—historical, political, spiritual, business, and so on—and then to discuss what admirable qualities are exhibited by these leaders. They can also state any other qualities that they feel are an important aspect of leadership. Allow 10 minutes for the brainstorming.

After 10 minutes, have each group report the leadership qualities it came up with. Neatly write each quality on the flip chart, using two or more pages if necessary. When writing on the flip chart, be sure to allow plenty of room in the left margin of the page.

Once all groups have finished reporting, tell employees that it's time to take a 15-minute break. At the break, employees should come up to the flip chart—one by one—and put their stickers next to the two qualities that they feel are *most* important. Doing this during a break allows employees to post their priorities more anonymously than if they had to do it in front of everyone else. Once this has been done by all employees, note which qualities were deemed as the most important.

Depending on your objectives, you may want to continue after the break with a discussion of how those qualities can be put into practice by the leaders at your organization. Alternatively, you can keep the flip-chart page(s) for your own education and share the information with the other leaders of the organization—for example, supervisors of your team and senior management.

Additional Ideas

- Get together with other managers—especially those who interact with your team—to discuss the results and look at ways to put the top priorities into practice in the daily work environment.

■ Keep the flip chart page(s) and in about six months revisit the activity with the group of employees. Ask if they feel that these leadership qualities are exhibited by managers in the organization.

■ Follow up this activity with a discussion of which qualities are *least* effective/desirable in a leader.

34
Quotation Quest

In a Nutshell

Employees read partial quotes by famous leaders and try to come up with the missing words. This fun, often comical, game is an ideal conversation-starter that also yields interesting insights about employees' perspectives.

Time

About 10–15 minutes. This should be done in a group session.

What You'll Need

Photocopies of the handout—one for every two or three employees. Participants will need pens.

What to Do

Put the employees into pairs or groups of three and give each group a copy of the handout. Tell them to make their best guess as to what the missing words are in each quotation. If there is more than one word missing, they will see more than one blank. The length of each blank is the same, however, regardless of the length of the missing word or words. If you feel it is necessary, remind employees to avoid writing anything offensive or inappropriate.

After about 7 minutes, go down the list of quotations and ask each group what words they inserted before giving them the correct answer for each one. (Answers appear below and on the following page.) Debrief by discussing what logic they applied to come up with their answers. You might also ask employees which quotation is their favorite, which ones they think are the most often true, who the people who authored the quotations are, and so on.

Additional Ideas

- You might expand the debrief portion of the game by asking employees to say more about the leadership provided by each of these individuals. Or, if they don't know, assign a few employees to find out three interesting facts about each individual and to report back to the group.

- Ask a few volunteers to create a bulletin board where employees can regularly post inspiring quotes (not necessarily on leadership).

Answers

1. "Be willing to make <u>decisions</u>. That's the most important quality in a good leader."   —*General George S. Patton Jr.*

2. "Leadership and <u>learning</u> are indispensable to each other." —*John F. Kennedy*

3. "As we look ahead into the next century, leaders will be those who <u>empower</u> others."   —*Bill Gates*

4. "Few things help an individual more than to place <u>responsibility</u> upon him and to let him know you <u>trust</u> him." —*Booker T. Washington*

5. "Leadership is the capacity to translate <u>vision</u> into reality." —*Warren Bennis*

6. "Nothing great was ever achieved without <u>enthusiasm</u>."
   —*Ralph Waldo Emerson*'

7. "<u>Nothing</u> gives one person so much <u>advantage</u> over another as to remain always cool and unruffled under any circumstances."   —*Thomas Jefferson*

8. "You can't build a reputation on what you're <u>going</u> <u>to</u> <u>do</u>." —*Henry Ford*

9. "The most pathetic person in the world is someone who has <u>sight</u> but has no vision."   —*Helen Keller*

10. "Never doubt that a <u>small</u> group of thoughtful, concerned citizens can change the <u>world</u>. Indeed it is the only thing that ever has."   —*Margaret Mead*

Quotation Quest

Instructions: Work with your partner(s) to fill in the blanks of the following quotations.

1. "Be willing to make _____. That's the most important quality in a good leader."   —*General George S. Patton Jr.*

2. "Leadership and _____ are indispensable to each other."   —*John F. Kennedy*

3. "As we look ahead into the next century, leaders will be those who _____ others."   —*Bill Gates*

4. "Few things help an individual more than to place _____ upon him and to let him know you _____ him."
   —*Booker T. Washington*

5. "Leadership is the capacity to translate _____ into reality."   —*Warren Bennis*

6. "Nothing great was ever achieved without _____."
   —*Ralph Waldo Emerson*

7. "_____ gives one person so much _____ over another as to remain always cool and unruffled under any circumstances."   —*Thomas Jefferson*

8. "You can't build a reputation on what you're _____ _____ _____."   —*Henry Ford*

9. "The most pathetic person in the world is someone who has _____ but has no vision."   —*Helen Keller*

10. "Never doubt that a _____ group of thoughtful, concerned citizens can change the _____. Indeed it is the only thing that ever has."   —*Margaret Mead*

35

Remembering Greatness

In a Nutshell

Employees recall a favorite leader from their past—teacher, coach, mentor, or manager—and describe why that person left such a lasting and favorable impression on the employee. This game gives leaders valuable insights into what leadership styles and actions have deeply inspired and affected employees.

Time

Approximately 10 minutes, but possibly longer if the group is large. This can easily be done as an individual activity as well.

What You'll Need

Nothing

What to Do

Ask participants to close their eyes for a minute or two and to reflect on the past. Thinking through their childhood, adolescence, and adulthood, they should identify one person in a position of leadership who left a strong, positive impression on them. It could be a teacher, a coach, a mentor, a previous manager, or anyone else. Tell them to think about not only *what* this person did but also *how* it affected the employee and why it was so effective and memorable.

After a few minutes, have each employee make a brief report.

Debrief by pointing out any patterns that you perceive in their reports. For example, often it's the little things that leave a lasting and positive impression, and it's the simplest and humblest leaders who make such a profound difference in people's lives.

Additional Ideas

■ This activity doesn't have to be done in a group setting. It works well as an open question in a conversation between manager and employee. It's also a great job-interview question.

■ One effective way to facilitate this activity is to have employees make their reports one at a time but at different points in the session (or even over the course of a week or longer). For example, announce the activity and then hear from one or two employees. At the next break, hear from one or two more. After lunch, ask another two, and so forth until everyone has had a turn.

Part Eight
WHAT YOU SAY AND WHAT YOU DON'T

Activities to improve your team's verbal and nonverbal communication

36

Three-Way Communication

In a Nutshell

Through some fun experiential learning, employees determine key aspects of communication in the face-to-face, phone, and e-mail environments.

Time

About 15 minutes. This is a group activity.

What You'll Need

A flip chart and marker, a few bandanas, a few clipboards, pens, and paper

What to Do

Preface the game with a brief discussion about the various ways in which employees communicate with their customers, colleagues, vendors, and other constituents. Tell them that in this activity, they will be determining key aspects and guidelines for three different communication methods: face-to-face, telephone, and e-mail.

Divide the employees into three groups. The first group represents the face-to-face environment. These people do not have any controls on their communication. They should sit in one area of the room and use pen and paper to write their findings during the activity.

The second group represents the telephone environment. These employees should be blindfolded with the bandanas in order to replicate the telephone environment (in which they cannot see the person they're talking to). They should sit together in one area of the room. One person will act as the scribe for the group's findings and will not wear a blindfold.

The third group represents the e-mail environment. These employees should sit back to back and may not speak. They should have paper, pens, and clipboards. In order to communicate, they must write notes and pass them to one another.

Now give all the groups their task: They should "discuss" the pros and cons of their communication method and come up with at least three guidelines for making communication via that method clear and positive.

Give them about 7 minutes and then ask each group to make its report. (Participants can now be free of the blindfolds, clipboards, and other constraints.)

Capture their findings and guidelines on a flip chart. After the session, transfer the information into a computer document and distribute a copy to all participants.

37

A Better Way to Say It

In a Nutshell

Employees practice some key skills for communication with coworkers when they are requesting help or information.

Time

About 15–20 minutes. This is a group activity.

What You'll Need

A flip chart, markers, and tape

What to Do

Work with the employees to brainstorm 10 to 15 common requests they make of one another in the course of their jobs. They might be requesting information, help, some tangible object, or anything else.

Capture the requests on a flip chart, writing one at the top of each page. Talk briefly about how the employees currently make these requests. What do they say? Do they make the request in person, over the phone, or via e-mail? Do they plan what they're going to say before they say it?

Next, tell the group that now they're going to learn two good luck charms for getting their requests fulfilled in a way that's professional, positive, and effective. In other words, they're going to learn that there's a better way to say it. The two practices are:

■ Ask; don't tell.

■ Show the value.

"Ask; don't tell" is pretty self-explanatory. This is a helpful way to frame a request because everyone likes to be asked rather than told to do something. "Show the value" means letting the other person know what benefit will be derived from fulfilling the request. They need to consider what the value is and then point it out to the other person. For example:

"Your expertise would really help this customer understand how her insurance plan works. Right now she's so confused."

"If I can get that paperwork from you by the end of today, we'll be able to meet the deadline for turning in our budget."

Divide the flip-chart pages into two sets and post each set in a different part of the room (creating two stations, each with at least five pages posted side by side). One station is the "Ask; don't tell" station and the other is the "Show the value" station.

Divide the group into two teams and assign each team to one of the two stations (they'll need markers). Their job is to come up with a "better way to say it" for each request and to write it out on the corresponding flip-chart page. After about 10 minutes, have each group present its requests. Debrief by discussing the following:

- It's sometimes not necessary to show the value (for example, if someone requested a book), but it's still an important skill to have for those times when it is necessary.

- Work is a nicer place to be if people treat each other with respect by asking instead of telling.

38

Attitude Charades

In a Nutshell

Employees act out various emotions and attitudes without using any words, as the rest of the group guesses what is being communicated.

Time

About 15 minutes. This is a group activity.

What You'll Need

A photocopy of the accompanying form, cut into strips (with one emotion on each), and a hat, bowl, or basket

What to Do

You might want to preface the game with a brief discussion about the importance of nonverbal communication. According to some studies, in the face-to-face environment more than 50 percent of the message conveyed comes through nonverbal communication. *What* is being said is no more important than *how* it is being said!

Spend a few moments brainstorming the various types of nonverbal communication. Be sure to include the following:

- Gestures

- Eye contact

- Body positions and movements

- Posture

- Facial expressions

- Proximity

- Energy level

Tell participants that they're now going to take turns acting out certain emotions (and attitudes), using only nonverbal communication, and everyone else has to guess what emotion is being conveyed. Put a chair at the front of the room so that each actor can choose to display the emotion either sitting or standing. Put the 12 strips of paper into the hat and have the first participant draw one and then act out the emotion. The audience should guess, and then the actor can reveal what emotion he or she was acting out. Continue until all the emotions have been acted out.

During the game, point out that some nonverbal communication can be used to convey more than one meaning.

Additional Ideas

- Follow up with a discussion of how the *voice* is used to convey emotions: through tone, pitch, volume, and so on.

- At some later time, you might want to create a reverse version of this game. You would list a number of nonverbal communication cues (a firm handshake, open-arm gestures, lowered eyes, etc.) and have employees act them out while everyone else says what that gesture means to them.

Attitude Charades

Photocopy this page and cut out each emotion. Fold the strips and put them into a hat for the Attitude Charades game.

Happiness

Grief

Anger

Frustration

Impatience

Sadness

Boredom

Arrogance

Indecision

Fear

Nervousness

Annoyance

39

 ## *Nix the Negativity*

In a Nutshell

Employees revise a series of negative statements in order to make them more positive and upbeat.

Time

About 10–15 minutes. This is a group activity but, with minor adjustment, can be turned into an individual activity.

What You'll Need

A list of several negative statements from your work environment (see below); a small, soft ball or stuffed animal. Employees will need pens.

What to Do

Preparation

For a few days (or a week or however long it takes), pay close attention to the language you hear employees use in the course of their work (the statements can come from exchanges with customers or with coworkers). Write down several examples of negative statements. You can also include statements that come across as overly demanding.

Following are a few examples, to give you an idea of what to listen for:

- Don't put that book there.

- We can't do that.

- That won't work.

- That's not our policy.

- You'll have to call back when you have the necessary information.

Write the statements on a sheet of paper, leaving enough space for employees to rewrite them during the group session. Make photocopies (one per employee) for the group session.

Note: If it will be obvious to employees—because of the context—who the speaker of a negative statement was, change the statement to assure anonymity. For example, if Betty is the only person who would say, "You must have your time sheets in by Friday," then change the statement to "You must have the paperwork in on time."

At the Group Session
Preface the game by briefly discussing the power of positive communication: when people speak in a positive, upbeat way, it builds rapport and increases collaboration.

Hand out the list of negative statements and tell employees that these are all statements that were recently overheard in the department/organization. Tell them that their job is to rewrite them and "nix the negativity." They should revise the statements to be more positive, collaborative, and upbeat. Give employees 7–10 minutes to rewrite.

Ask everyone to stand up. Tell the group that you're going to toss the ball to someone, and that person should read both the negative statement and the rewrite and then throw the ball back to you. If you want to hear additional rewrites, pass the ball to a couple more people. Do this for each of the negative statements.

Note: If you want to make this an individual activity, give each employee a copy of the list and ask everyone to revise the statements and then return the sheet to you to review.

40

Five Seconds to a First Impression

In a Nutshell

Employees look at a several pictures of individuals and then discuss what impressions they get in just five seconds.

Time

For you, this activity requires some preparation that may take 20–30 minutes. In the group session, the activity takes no more than 10 minutes. It can be adapted for individuals.

What You'll Need

Using Microsoft PowerPoint software or a comparable program, create 10 to 15 overheads, each showing a photograph or clip art graphic of a person with whom participants could conceivably meet in a business setting. Look for a variety of clothing styles, facial expressions, ages, and other nonverbal clues. You will also need an overhead projector, a screen, and a watch with a second hand (or a digital watch). Participants will need pen and paper.

If you don't feel up to the technical challenge of creating the presentation, look through several magazines for photographs of individuals (not famous or recognizable people). The presentation will be a little less slick if done this way, but the learning objective will still be achieved.

What to Do

Preface the activity with a brief discussion about the importance of a first impression. Ask participants if they have any "first impression" anecdotes and tell them that conventional wisdom holds that the first few seconds of an initial meeting are the most important in terms of forming an impression in the other person's mind.

Tell participants that you're going to show them a series of pictures and they'll have only five seconds to look at the picture. They must then write down at least two adjectives that came to their mind about the person. They won't even have the benefit of hearing the person speak. Their impressions will come only through visual clues such as posture, gestures, clothing, facial expressions, and the like.

In order to maintain professionalism and integrity, participants should avoid citing anything about what they feel are the individuals' cultural, racial, or religious backgrounds. Instead, they should focus only on what each person is conveying during that five-second glimpse.

Show the overheads, keeping each one visible for only five seconds. After each one, ask members of the group for their impressions. What did they feel the person was consciously or unconsciously communicating through the visual presentation?

Debrief by discussing what kind of first impression participants think *they* make on customers, vendors, colleagues, management, and others. Do they consciously strive to make a good impression? What about first impressions that come via the telephone or e-mail?

Part Nine

JUST FOR FUN

Activities to alleviate stress and increase fun in the workplace

41

Before the Sun Goes Down

In a Nutshell

Employees focus on one thing they have to look forward to before the end of the day. This is a quick, energizing activity that can be done anytime you want to instantly lift the mood and refocus employees' mind-sets to be more positive.

Time

Just a few seconds per employee. This activity can be done as part of a group session or as an individual energizer whenever necessary.

What You'll Need

Nothing

What to Do

Ask employees to think of one thing that they have to look forward to before the end of the day. It can relate to work, family, recreation, or anything else. Also, it can be something big or small. The objective is to remind employees that there is always *something* to look forward to in their immediate future. Here are some examples:

- Going out to dinner

- Spending time with family or friends

- Closing a deal or finishing a project at work

- Exercising

- Talking to a long-distance friend on the phone or via e-mail

- Reading a book

- Watching a favorite television show

When prompted to focus on something positive, people often realize that every day a number of good things happen in their lives.

Additional Idea

- You can expand this game by asking employees to come up with one thing they're looking forward to in the next week, month, or year.

42

Name Droppers

In a Nutshell

Working in small groups, employees use the letters of their names to come up with a range of words and phrases. Although this is mostly a just-for-fun game, it does challenge employees to think quickly and creatively.

Time

Typically about 10–15 minutes. This is a group activity.

What You'll Need

One copy of the handout for every four participants. Participants will need pens and probably some scratch paper. You may want to get some small prizes to present to the winning team and to others (see Additional Ideas). Put the example ("THOMAS" and "BARBARA") on a flip chart or white board.

What to Do

Divide employees into groups of four. Distribute one copy of the handout to each group, and go over the instructions. First, all members of each group will write their first names on the lines provided. They'll then have 10 minutes to use these letters to come up with as many standard English words and phrases as they can in 10 minutes. They do not have to use every letter every time. They will probably want to designate one person on the team to be the scribe (the others can participate orally). Alternatively, they can each use scratch paper first and then combine lists onto the handout.

Review the example on the flip chart or white board:

THOMAS   BARBARA

RAT   BAR   MAT   RAM

TAR   BAT   SAT   HAT

Let employees know that the groups will be competing with one another.

Allow 10 minutes for them to play, and then ask each group for its results. Congratulate all participants for their creativity and quick thinking, and give out the prizes if you got them.

Additional Ideas

- Give additional prizes for words of four or more letters, and/or for the longest word or phrase that a group develops.

- After the game, ask if any of the groups developed a special technique for quickly coming up with new words and phrases.

Name Droppers

Using all capital letters, write the first names of the four people on your team on the lines below. Then move all the letters around to come up with as many standard English words or phrases as you can in 10 minutes. For each new word or phrase, you can use each letter only once. You do not have to use every letter every time. Names of people do not count as words, but names of countries and places, for example, do count as words.

Your names:

_____   _____

_____   _____

New words and phrases:

_____

_____

_____

_____

_____

_____

_____

_____

_____

_____

_____

43
Job Titles in Jest

In a Nutshell

Employees have fun coming up with fictional job titles for themselves, using a variety of quirky and impressive words.

Time

About 10–15 minutes. This can be an individual activity, but it is much more fun in a group setting. If you have employees do it on their own, be sure to have them tell others what title they've chosen.

What You'll Need

One copy of the handout for each employee. Tent cards (or 8½" × 11" sheets of card stock folded lengthwise)—one per employee—and markers.

What to Do

Note: This is a great activity to do early on in a group session, so employees can display their tent cards for the duration of the session.

Tell employees that they are now going to have an opportunity to be an executive, a magician, a chieftain, or anything else they want to be. Give everyone a copy of the handout, a tent card, and a marker. Allow them 5 minutes to come up with their new job titles and to write them on their tent cards.

After 5 minutes, ask all participants to present their job titles and to display their tent cards. Ask each employee for a brief explanation of why and how he or she chose that title.

For added fun, have the employees confer—either in small groups or in one large group—to come up with a fun job title for you.

Job Titles in Jest

Use any of the titles below, combined with some aspect of your actual job, to come up with a new job title. If you don't see anything you like, dream up something else. This one is just for fun!

Examples: High Priest of Programming, Minister of Mischief

Alchemist	High Priest
Captain	Leader
Yogi	President
Chairman/Chairwoman	Abbot/Abbess
Charioteer	Conductor
Producer	Guide
Pilot	Shepherd
Director	Chieftain
Chief	Head
Master	Ambassador
King/Queen	Dreamer
Prince/Princess	Warden
Minister	Commander
Superintendent	Grand Marshal
Taskmaster/Taskmistress	Champion
Emperor/Empress	Sprite
Wizard	Magician
Monk	Patriarch/Matriarch
Hierarch	Bestower

44

Humor in the Air

In a Nutshell

Employees share humorous anecdotes in a unique and surprising way.

Time

The on-your-own part of this activity takes place over a day or two. Then, in the group session, the second part of the activity takes 5–10 minutes.

What You'll Need

Enough sheets of 8½″ × 11″ paper, in various colors, for each employee

What to Do

A day or two before the group session, give each employee a sheet of the colored paper and ask everyone to find a clean joke, a humorous anecdote, a funny picture, or the like. Employees can use something they've heard, look in a joke book, ask a child, get on the Internet, or find it somewhere else. Anything goes, as long as it will make people laugh and will fit on a sheet of paper. Employees should copy the humorous tidbit onto the sheet of paper and then bring it to the group session. They should not share it with anyone before the session.

At the group session, whenever it's time for an injection of energy and humor, ask everyone to take his or her piece of paper and make a paper airplane out of it. Then tell them that on the count of three, they should all stand up and send their paper airplanes into the air. Yell out, "One-two-three!"

Once all the paper airplanes have been flown, everyone should pick up one that is a different color from his or her own. One by one, have employees unfold the airplanes and read what's written or show everyone the picture.

45
Flip-Chart Frenzy

In a Nutshell

Employees quickly rotate to various stations where they offer serious and not-so-serious ideas for one another. This is a fun way to share ideas, energize a group session, and gain insight into the likes and dislikes of employees.

Time

This activity requires some minor preparation on your part. For the group session, allow about 10 minutes.

What You'll Need

Flip-chart paper, tape, markers (preferably, in several colors) for all participants, a watch with a second hand, and, ideally, a whistle

What to Do

Preparation

Before the group session, choose several topics and write each one at the top of a flip-chart page. Try to have as many pages as you have employees, but if this is not feasible, then people can rotate into and out of the game. Each topic should be simple and self-explanatory; participants will have to immediately comprehend what they are supposed to write and will have only seconds to do so.

The possibilities are endless and, of course, depend on the type of information you're looking for. I recommend you alternate between fun, frivolous topics and meatier ones that will give you insight into employees' opinions and emotions. Following are a few suggestions—of both types—to get you started:

- A great local restaurant

- Biggest challenge facing our team

- Favorite travel destination

- Idea for a new employee benefit

- Best movie of all time

- Suggestion for increasing sales

- How you would spend a "found" hundred-dollar bill

- One thing you like about working here

- Favorite book

- Training/education you would like

At the Group Session
Post all the prepared flip-chart pages at various spots around the room. Tape the bottom of each page to the top so that, for now, the topic cannot be seen. Give each participant a marker, and go over the instructions for the game:

1. You will each start at one station and then rotate counterclockwise each time I blow the whistle. (*Note*: If you don't have a whistle, you can clap loudly or yell out, "Rotate.")

2. At each station, write an answer and then put your initials next to it.

3. You will have only a short visit at each station, so write the first thing that comes to your mind.

4. Do not rotate to the next station until I have told you to.

Assign everyone to a station and start the game. Allow only 20–30 seconds at each station. Continue until all participants have visited each station.

After the game, briefly review the answers to see if any patterns exist and to let everyone benefit from the shared information (restaurant and movie recommendations, etc.). Discuss the ideas however you see fit. You might want to point out that often the best ideas come not through extended consideration, but through spontaneous inspiration.

Take the flip-chart pages with you after the session, so that you can more closely review the responses to the work-related topics. Be sure to let employees know about any changes you make based on their feedback during the game.

Part Ten

ON YOUR OWN

Solo activities for the leader to do

46

Walk the Talk

In a Nutshell

This two-part exercise helps managers translate intentions into actions. It's an effective on-your-own activity that uncovers important aspects of one's management style.

Time

About 15–20 minutes. This is an individual activity.

What You'll Need

One photocopy each of Walk the Talk Work Sheet 1 and Work Sheet 2

What to Do

It's always nice to say that you're committed to supporting and empowering your employees, but it's equally important to show that you mean it. How do you do that? You do it through your management style and the actions you take on a daily basis to support and empower your team.

Complete Work Sheets 1 and 2, and then complete the most important step of all: putting these actions into practice in your real-time environment.

Walk the Talk Work Sheet 1

Take a few moments to think about the various functions of your employees' jobs and about your management style. Despite what you say or what you intend, what are the messages you actually communicate to employees? Write down two actions or habits that tend to be patterns in your management style and that you suspect may be sending the wrong messages to employees. Next, decipher those actions by asking yourself what messages they actually convey to your employees—despite what your intention is. Here's an example:

Action 1: I don't look at people when they are talking to me. Instead, I look down at the floor or off in the distance.

What it says: I can't give you my full attention. I have other things on my mind. I find it uncomfortable to look directly at you.

Action 1: _____

_____

_____

What it says: _____

_____

_____

Action 2: _____

_____

_____

What it says: _____

_____

_____

Walk the Talk Work Sheet 2

Once you've completed Work Sheet 1, try coming up with some messages that you do want to convey to employees and then translate them into specific actions. For example:

What I want to convey: I know it's often very hard to stay motivated and energetic.

Actions that convey this message: Smiles, words of encouragement, personal stories from my experiences "in the trenches," reminding employees of previous successes

What I want to convey: _____

_____

Actions that convey this message: _____

_____

What I want to convey: _____

_____

Actions that convey this message: _____

_____

Stumped about what messages to convey through your actions? Here are a few suggestions:

- "I trust you."

- "I value your contribution."

- "You're a professional."

- "I'm aware of your presence and of the work you do."

47

The Practice of Praise

In a Nutshell

This activity encourages the leader to regularly praise his or her employees and offers tips and techniques for making this a valuable, mutually rewarding experience.

Time

Time varies. This is a solo activity for the manager.

What You'll Need

Nothing but a strong willingness to see your employees do well!

What to Do

Let's start with a pop quiz. Have you praised an employee in the last day or two? And the day or two before that? Is your praise specific (so that the employee knows what, exactly, he or she should continue doing)? Do you praise *all* your employees, but make the praise unique for each one? Is your praise delivered sincerely, and without sarcasm or cynicism? Do you find real things to praise, rather than just trivial things (that might then make your employees suspicious of your motives)? Do you feel better at the end of the day and the end of the week when you've made a conscious effort to highlight the good things that are happening in your department and to recognize those employees who are responsible?

OK, here are the correct answers to the pop quiz: yes, yes, yes, yes, yes, yes, and yes. Good for you if you got them all right! (If you didn't, keep reading and then take the quiz again next week.)

Following are a few ideas to help keep the practice of praising your employees fresh, rewarding, and meaningful:

- Put four coins in your right pocket (or on the right side of your desk). Every time you praise an employee, move one coin over to your left pocket (or left side of your desk). Every morning and every afternoon, try to transfer all four coins.

- Create a reproducible form with an alphabetized list of your employees on it. At the beginning of each workweek, start with a clean copy. As you go through the week, highlight each name to indicate that you've praised that individual for something. Try to have every name highlighted by the end of each week.

- Using small sheets of paper, write a note of praise for each employee. Before anyone comes in to work, tape the notes under employees' chairs. At some point in the day, send out a group e-mail telling all employees to look under their chairs.

- Every week or two, select some aspect of your team's work that deserves a pat on the back. Send an e-mail or a voice mail to the group praising members for their collective success.

- Make the first thing and last thing you do every workday be to praise someone for a job well done.

48

Boss's Blueprint

In a Nutshell

The manager tests his or her familiarity with the work environment and with the individualities of employees.

Time

Time varies. This is a solo activity for the manager.

What to Do

Sit at your desk and take out a pen and a sheet of paper. Without looking around, draw a basic floor plan of the work environment that you manage. What is the layout? Who works where? Where are common-use items such as printers and copy machines located? Where are the windows and walls?

Once you've drawn the general design, start to fill in as many meaningful details as you can. Don't worry about insignificant things, but do pay attention to personal effects that give you insights into the minds and hearts of your employees. For example, what photos are on their desks? What art do they have in their work areas? What quotations have they posted to motivate themselves? What awards or accolades are on display?

This activity is designed to tell you two things about your management style. The first is to inform you of how well you know your employees' work environment. The second is to give you valuable information that can help you understand the individual characteristics and motivations of your staff.

Additional Idea

- Go out into the work area of your employees and look for opportunities to improve the physical environment. Are there any cluttered areas that could be cleaned up? Where would it help to put a plant, a little paint, or some other improvement?

49

Me, Myself, and My Leadership

In a Nutshell

Leaders write their own (fictional) retirement party tribute, highlighting key aspects of their career and leadership style. This activity gets the leader to think honestly about the perceptions of subordinates, and it focuses the leader's attention on what needs to be changed and what does not.

Time

Time varies, but probably at least 30 minutes

What You'll Need

A computer (or pen and paper)

What to Do

Although your retirement may be many years away, it's never too early to think about the impression you're making on your employees and about the feelings they will have about you when that retirement celebration finally comes! This activity is just between you and you. It might take you a little time to warm up to the idea—all of us are a little uncomfortable praising ourselves—but the end result will be an inspiring and eye-opening account about the direction of your leadership. So, go on, give it a try!

Imagine yourself seated at your own retirement party. Someone who has worked for you for many years stands up and goes to the podium to offer a tribute to you. What is said? What is not said? Your job is to write the tribute that you *want* to hear. Following are a few ideas to get you started:

- Highlight at least three specific characteristics of your leadership style and identify what effect each one has had on subordinates.

- Point out two or three key success stories from your career.

- Mention some challenges that you or your team have faced, and describe how your leadership overcame them.

- Point out which of your subordinates have flourished at least in part because of you.

- This is your opportunity to visualize, imagine, and dream!

And Then What?

Here are a few ideas for what to do when you've finished your tribute:

- Translate your imaginary tribute into reality. What specific actions do you need to take in order to change the direction or style of your leadership in the way that you want to? What tools and/or support do you need? How can you get them?

- If you're feeling brave, talk candidly about your leadership with trusted subordinates and/or with your spouse (or significant other) or a good friend. Now that you know what impression you *want* to have on people, be open to feedback from people close to you.

- Put the tribute away for a few months or even longer, and then review it. Ask yourself what has changed, what hasn't, what should, and what should not.

50

To Be or Not to Be

In a Nutshell

Leaders develop two lists—one describing what they *always* want to be and one describing what they *never* want to be. This is a simple but illuminating exercise that helps leaders to develop a sense of mission and to establish priorities for their professional lives.

Time

Time varies, but typically about 10 minutes

What You'll Need

A computer (or pen and paper)

What to Do

The premise of this on-your-own activity is very simple: you create two lists to help guide your actions and philosophy as a leader. The execution of the exercise, however, is often an unexpectedly poignant experience. Take a look at the sample lists and then take some time to reflect on your own values and priorities as a leader.

I suggest that you limit each of your lists to seven or fewer items. This will force you to decide which traits are most important to you. Plus, it's a manageable number. Having any more makes it difficult for you—or anyone—to sincerely commit to these values. And don't feel that you have to list seven items. If you feel that there are really only three things that are highly important to you, then just put those three on your list. It's *your* list!

One more tip: Avoid putting direct opposites on your lists. For example, if you put "fair" on your Always list, don't put "unfair" on your Never list.

Once you've finished, keep your lists close at hand so you'll refer to them often in the course of your daily work. They can serve a similar purpose to that of a mission statement if you remember to keep them in your mind and heart at all times.

Additional Ideas

- Try another round of this activity, but this time substitute the verb "do" for "be." You'll end up with lists of things you *always* and *never* want to do.

- Expand this activity to your personal life. What do you *always* and *never* want to be outside of work?

- Review and revise your lists from time to time. And be sure to reward yourself for your progress or outright success.

- You can try another variation of this activity by creating lists titled "These things are indispensable in my life" and "These things are entirely dispensable in my life." It's a great way to articulate your personal values. Once you've given it a try, encourage your employees to do the same thing for themselves.

Sample Lists for To Be or Not to Be

These things I *always* want to be:

1. Creative

2. Hardworking

3. Open-minded

4. Aspiring

5. Inspiring

These things I *never* want to be:

1. Unfair

2. Arrogant

3. Lethargic

About the Author

Vasudha K. Deming has been active in the field of training and development since 1992 as an instructional designer, author, trainer, and consultant. She is the coauthor of *Managing and Motivating Contact Center Employees*, *The Big Book of Customer Service Training Games*, and *The Big Book of Sales Games*. A resident of San Diego, she is a director at Impact Learning Systems, a California-based company that specializes in helping organizations to create positive work environments and to master interpersonal communication skills.